# PUSSYCATS NEED LOVE, TOO

# GEORGE BOOTH

# PUSSYCATS NEED LOVE, TOO

**AVON**
PUBLISHERS OF BARD, CAMELOT, DISCUS AND FLARE BOOKS

Of the 108 drawings in this book, 92 appeared originally in *The New Yorker* and were copyrighted © 1976, 1977, 1978, 1979, and 1980 by the New Yorker Magazine, Inc.


AVON BOOKS
A division of
The Hearst Corporation
959 Eighth Avenue
New York, New York 10019

The Dodd, Mead and Company edition contains the following
Library of Congress Cataloging in Publication Data:

Booth, George, date
Pussycats need love, too.
1. American wit and humor, Pictorial.    I. Title.
NC1429.B666A4      1980      741.5'973

First Avon Printing, September, 1981

For
The National Lyric Opera Company
5332 Sherier Place, N.W.
Washington, D.C. 20016

*Franks and beans.*

*"Hey, guys, you know what?"*

"You can _not_ 'miss July,' Miss Dunwoodie, because your loan is
a pay-every-month loan, not a miss-a-month loan."

"*I'll have the 'Tomato Oh My Gosh,' please.*"

"*Oh my gosh!*"

*"Tony asked me to ask you, Mr. Bates—do you know offhand the whereabouts of your service manual?"*

BOOTH.

*Avoid overstimulation.*

*Reserve a few minutes each morning to recall the halcyon days of youth.*

*Spend more time alone.*

Putter among the flowers before breakfast.

Take catnaps whenever you can.

Every now and then, drop a few dirty dishes in the disposal.

Stay single.

BOOTH

"I'm sitting here going over all my troubles in my mind, and there's Ferguson over yonder, a man utterly at peace with himself. Then suddenly—*whack! whoopty-do!*— his rocker snaps, and it's off the north end of the porch with him! How about that?"

"*Julia Child was cooking coq au vin and tambour parmentier this evening, and during her pommes en belle vue I burned your filet.*"

"*The United States Congress is urging all of us to produce more.*"

*"Like my cowboy clogs?"*

"*You are not entitled to the Cuisinart food processor in this category, Miss Dunwoodie. You are entitled to the Patty Cake stuffed monkey.*"

*"Yeeaah!" "Yeeaah!" "Yeeaah!" "Yeeaah!" "Yeeaah!"*

"*Yeeeeeaaaaah!*"

BOOTH.

"*Mrs. Ritterhouse says if you want to buy fresh seed clams, rendezvous tonight at midnight one block north of the Fulton Fish Market. Pass it on.*"

"*Newspaper reporters always describe Hereford as unflappable.
Newspaper reporters don't live with Hereford. I do. He's not.*"

*"Now, see here!"*

"We located the hissing noise, Mr. Watkins. Your wife's mother is in the back seat."

*"Last night I heard a cicada."*

BOOTH.

"I'm going to send you down the hall to see Dr. Hunseth.
And please tell Dr. Hunseth it's his turn to send one of
his patients to me."

*"Last call for stuffed peppers or I feed 'em to the dog!"*

BOOTH.

# MARRIAGE

Young ladies, prior to marriage, must stay ready.

Take it easy with the after-shave.

Introduce some fresh ideas into your sex life.

Grow together.

There is much loose talk going around about polygamy. Ignore it.

For better or for worse, support your spouse.

*In the ideal marriage both partners are vulnerable.*

*Take time to fall in love again.*

*Remember: Some people are not marriageable.*

BOOTH.

"The beans with chili, the businessman's teriyaki lunch, and the
tomato stuffed with egg salad are dangerous today."

*"The Armentrout brothers never achieved much success in the business world, but they <u>have</u> caught <u>lots</u> of butterflies."*

"*She's all set, Mr. Ferguson, but don't go yet. We've got to get Rizzo loose. His coveralls are snagged on her tailpipe bracket.*"

"We may as well go home. It's obvious that this meeting isn't going to settle anything."

"*Mr. Swinehart has just crossed Route 36 at Goshen Junction. We are all expected, in exactly eighteen minutes, to greet him as he comes down the driveway.*"

"*My mother always says that. She always says, 'You have to be a little bit crazy to live in New York.' Mother is a little crazy, but she doesn't live in New York. She lives in Nishnabotna, Missouri.*"

BOOTH

*"Hendershot, there, does his best to keep smiling."*

*"Not dogs today, Coontz! Today is piano music!"*

"*Bernard, a Lieutenant Colonel Lucy Treadwell, of Consumer Vigilantes, Fox Company, 2nd Batallion, Utilities Division, wants to know do we have any complaints in regard to our utility services.*"

*"Old Jesse located your trouble, Mr. Watkins, but he won't tell us what it is until after the ice-cream truck comes."*

*"Attention, please, Mr. Lyle Ferguson. As a result of equipment failure at the Cos Cob power station, your train will not be running at all tonight."*

*"How often, might I ask, does the World Saxophone Congress meet?"*

*"By Jupiter, an angel! Or, if not, an earthly paragon!"*

*"Sometimes Dunnehee hears the croak of his first wife."*

BOOTH

"*Pegler drank a toast to Mrs. Pegler, then he drank a toast to each of Mrs. Pegler's thirteen cats. That's too damn many cats!*"

"*It's sixteen hundred dollars for August, including gas, electricity, maintenance, beach sticker, and old Mrs. Pennington up in the attic.*"

"Are they still fighting organized crime or have they decided to let it alone?"

*Eleven dogs on a porch.*

"Biggers, two more Luau Sizzlers for Annie and me and another
Fog Cutter for Mrs. Grindstaff."

"*Your Big Jumbo, Roy, is your regular Jumbo with golden French fries and coleslaw. Your Super Jumbo is your Big Jumbo with slice of onion, lettuce, tomato, special dressing, and pickle wedge. I've been watching you, Roy. You're screwing up on the pickle wedge.*"

"*There goes Daddy to the park again! And do you know what he does in the park? He sits! That's what he does. He sits! He goes to the park and just sits!*"

*"Remember the Babylonian ziggurat?"*

BOOTH

"See that dog, Mr. Hendricks? That means you either have a shredded
fan belt or your fuel pump is sucking air."

BOOTH

BOOTH

"*Mrs. Van Lewis-Smythe, third wife of your chairman of the board, said to me this evening at the corporate hoodingy, and twenty people within earshot, 'We all know what <u>Mr.</u> Parmalee does. He is a very important vice-president of the Hi Lee Lolly Corporation. What we are all wondering, Mrs. Parmalee, is . . . just what is it that <u>you</u> do? Do you do anything?' I said, 'Mrs. Van Lewis-Smythe, Your Grace, I fix dripping faucets around our house. I prop up sagging bookshelves. I glue broken china. I clean windows, mirrors, floors, walls, pots and pans, and dishes. I jiggle the doodads on running toilets. I repair and refinish furniture. I cane chairs. I paint and sew. I do electrical work, drive nails, saw boards, and I give birth to our babies. I wash and iron and make the beds. I prepare the meals. I get the children to school. I trim the hedge, plant and maintain a vegetable garden and flower garden. I mow the lawn, clean the basement, feed the birds, the cats, a dog, and a chicken, <u>and</u> I chauffeur a very important vice-president of the Hi Lee Lolly Corporation to and from the bar car every blessed day.'*"

*"It's Monday night, hon—time for trivia quiz!"*

Buttons. A group can get together and have one person do the buying.

Fruits and nuts can be dried at home in your spare time

Peat.

Dirt-pushing machines.
Americans _need_ to push dirt.

Bedsprings. Double your worth.

BOOTH.

If all else fails, improve
your relationship with your in-laws.

"*It's not cotton, honey. It's nylon quilted to polyester. The leaves and trim are twenty per cent acrylic and eighty per cent modacrylic, and the flowers are acetate. The backing is polypropylene. Go to bed.*"

*"Bavoom!"*

*"Papa doesn't want Tsi Tsu in the bedroom while he's hiding his little nest egg."*

PROTECT THE WILDLIFE

*"He's nuts. She's nuts. All three young ones are nuts. The dog
is nuts. And the old lady upstairs is nuts, too."*

BOOTH.

"That metallic grinding means her throwout bearings are shot. She's backfiring through her carburetor. The tick indicates transmission trouble, and the smoke means she's on fire."

*"Crippling local, state, and federal rules and regulations have made criminals out of many a small businessman, Ma'am."*

"Broadbent has donated a philodendron to the club every year
for twenty-eight years. Broadbent is a good old boy."

*"Forgive me for the horrible thing I have done."*

*"Forgive me for the horrible thing I have done."*

BOOTH

*"Thank you for not smoking."*

*"My son Ronald begins to open up around eight o'clock in the evening.
His best hours are from then until along about sunup, when he wilts
and drops off like a night-blooming cereus."*

"*As for me and Bertie here, we will endeavor, in the face of constantly rising costs, to maintain our criteria of excellence. Ain't that right, Bertie?*"

"*Once it catches on, the small-horse household-pet idea will go like blazes. And you may quote Mr. Pudney on that.*"

"*I feel aggressive today. Not sexy—just aggressive.*"

*"My fellow-employees, it is my painful duty to tell you that discovery of a cash shortage was made this morning amounting to some eighteen million dollars."*

BOOTH

*"Thank you for your prompt cooperation."*

*"Uncle Alstaire says it's going to be a 'three-dog night.'"*

*"Mister Ferguson's not here. He's away. He's split
this joint. Twenty-three skidoo. Gone bye-bye."*

BOOTH.

"She's going to run you a bit of money this time. Your entire ignition syst
undergone what our chief mechanic, Mr. Murchison, terms a 'core meltdo

*"Leader Maloop, the people yearn for real answers."*

" 'The difference _you_ make makes _all_ the difference.' Well put!"

"Perhaps the Mesopotamians abandoned the reed vessel at this
juncture, Professor, and continued by dhow?"

*"Before the break is over, I'm going to introduce you to our first violinist, Mrs. Ritterhouse. After one has had a good long talk with Mrs. Ritterhouse, all the barnacles let loose and fall off and one sits higher in the water. Here, have another watercress sandwich."*

BOOTH

"*Gram isn't one to say 'I told you so.' But if you recollect your wedding day some thirty-odd years ago, Gram did say you weren't getting the biggest slice of pie in town.*"

"*If you can't get Riley to talk to you, Mr. Henderson, don't worry about it.
He'll still fix your fuel pump. Riley, fix Mr. Henderson's fuel pump.*"

*"She's just like her mother!"*

*"Since the CB-radio boom, Mother Cantwell's dental work has been receiving <u>and</u> sending."*

*"Tick-tick," "Tick-tick," "Tick-tick," "Tick-tick," "Tick-tick," "Tick-tick," "Tick-tick," "Tick-tick," "Tick-tick," "Tick-tick," "Tick-tick."*

*"Cuckoo," "Cuckoo," "Cuckoo," "Cuckoo," "Cuckoo," "Cuckoo," "Cuckoo," "Cuckoo," "Cuckoo," "Cuckoo," "Cuckoo," "Cuckoo."*

*"Lord A'mighty!"*

"*Templeton has been catching crappies all morning on a jig. He snagged a seven-pound bass on a Mississippi silverside minnow, and now he's after a monstrous channel cat with a stinkball. You'd better wake him before he goes over the limit.*"

"*I know what I want for Christmas! I want one of those itty-bitty toolboxes that have an eentsy-weentsy screwdriver and an eentsy-weentsy hammer and an eentsy-weentsy pair of pliers and on the lid is the cutest eentsy-weentsy beentsy-teentsy tiny little padlock and key!*"

*"You got here just in time, Mr. Lundquist. The boys are ready
to give your transmission the gang gong."*

*"Chicken with forty cloves of garlic! How does that sound?"*

BOOTH

*"One of you boys go help Mom with the groceries."*